CRAFTS
Quilting
and
Patchwork

© 1992 Lyric Books Ltd
PO Box 152, Mill Hill, London NW7, England

First published in 1992

ISBN 0 7111 0017 9

Printed in Belgium by
Proost International Book Production

Introduction

HARMONY CLASS is for everyone. Beginners will find it friendly and instructional, experienced knitters will find it challenging and informative.

Step-by-step instructions for some of the most common appliqué techniques are followed by the pattern for making a Baby's Quilt.

The Quilt pattern is the basis for an unlimited number of design variations that can be made by using different fabrics and and changing the motifs that are appliquéd. In the third section we have given you all the letters of the alphabet plus the numerals zero to nine. Included with these are a few suggestions of ways to decorate the letters and different designs to inspire you, but remember - **the choice is yours**.

Basic sewing and embroidery techniques, which will be of particular interest to the less experienced person, follow and we finish with some hints and tips which could be helpful to all of you.

Incidentally, we would be glad to hear from **you** if you have tips which we can add to future editions of our books and which would interest others.

Contents

Appliqué . . . . page 3
Pattern and Designs . . . . page 9
Design Variations . . . . page 12
Sewing Know How . . . . page 38
Top of the Class . . . . page 48

Appliqué

Appliqué is the art of applying one fabric to another, by hand or machine stitchery, with or without added embroidery. It is one of the quickest and easiest kinds of needlecraft, creating a rewarding effect with a minimum of sewing. It is a very adaptable technique with can be used for many kinds of practical and decorative projects.

Motifs applied by machine stitching can be used to decorate quilts and garments and this kind of applied work will stand up well to hard wear and washing.

Choice of Fabrics

A firm, closely woven fabric of medium weight is best for backgrounds. Avoid fabrics that stretch or fray. The easiest fabrics to apply are felt, leather and other non-woven fabrics. However, by using special iron-on nylon bonding webs most fabrics can be made non-fraying nowadays with a little advance preparation.

For practical items, choose colourfast and washable fabrics and make sure that the applied pieces and the background fabric are the same type and weight.

Threads

Use cotton or silk threads for natural fibres and synthetic thread for man-made fibres. It helps to unify a design if different shapes and colours are all applied with the same colour of thread. In general, the thread should be unobtrusive when used for the actual appliqué, although all kinds of threads may be used for added embroidery.

Edge Treatment

This should be considered at the design stage. Edges can be treated so that the stitchery is invisible, they can be machined over to make a strong line or embroidered over so that the edge shades off into the background. Each method gives a different emphasis to the design.

Designs

Appliqué design is based on bold and simple shapes like the letters of the alphabet and numbers given on pages 14 to 34. Designs can also be based on folded paper cut-outs, simple geometric shapes like circles and squares, abstract motifs, or natural ones like sprays of flowers. The shapes can be arranged symmetrically, singly or overlapped.

Transferring Designs

The design motifs can be transferred in a number of ways. Card templates may be used or tracings can be made through dressmakers carbon.

To Make a Template

Trace or draw a separate motif for each part of the design you wish to apply on thick paper or thin card using carbon paper to help you. Remember to include any markings such as stitching lines.

Cut out the traced shape which is then called a **template**. No allowance for turnings is included on card templates as a rule.

Methods of Work

Bascially, there are three different ways of working simple appliqué.

Firstly, there is the machine sewn method where the fabric to be applied

is pinned, tacked then sewn by machine to the background fabric.

Secondly, there is the traditional method whereby the background fabric is framed up, the applied pieces are cut (with turnings if the fabric tends to fray) and the pieces pinned, tacked and hand sewn in place.

If the fabric is non-woven, for instance felt, turnings are not required.

Thirdly, there is the quick and easy no-sew method using one of the special bonding webs. This material is sold in small packs and can be obtained from haberdashery sections of department stores and fabric retailers. Here, the design motifs are ironed straight on to the background.

Preparation of the Background Fabric

Always iron the fabric before starting work. Then, using chalk lines or a row of pins or tacking, mark centre lines on the fabric from top to bottom and side to side. Use these marks to position the motifs.

Preparation of the Motif

Lay the template on the applied fabric in such a way that when the motif is laid on the background the grain direction of both fabrics will match. Unless the fabric is a non-woven one, remember to add a 6 mm [1/4 inch] seam allowance all round if using the

hand sewn method. Either hold the fabric and template firmly together and cut round the template, or trace round the template with a dressmakers pencil and then cut the fabric out along the line.

Machine Sewn Method

Position the motif on to the background fabric, matching the grain of the fabrics and pin in place at right angles to the outline. Either machine or hand tack round the outline near to the edge, then using a close zig-zag stitch machine over the raw edges.

If you do not have a sewing machine, or if you prefer, you can embroider over the raw edge with satin stitch (see page 47).

Zig-Zag Stitch

The larger the number on the stitch length dial (or lever) the wider apart the stitches become. If a long length of stitch is used, then the zig-zag is very open. As the length is reduced the stitch closes up until it becomes satin stitch.

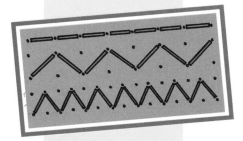

The length of the stitch operates the closeness of the zig-zag.

Turning Corners

Try to avoid overlapping on corners as this causes the stitching to pile up. The following method is better:

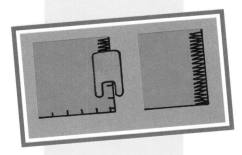

1 Work to the corner, stop with the needle on the inside of the shape (left-hand side) in the fabric.

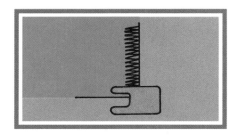

2 Lift the foot, turn the corner, put the foot down again - it is now off the shape. Use the drive wheel by hand to move the needle away from the fabric.

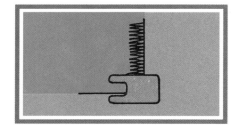

3 Lift the presser foot and slide the shape back into line with the needle.

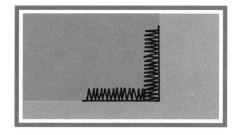

4 Lower the foot and continue stitching.

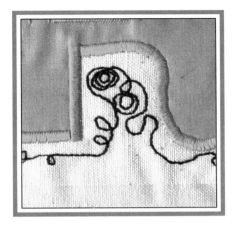

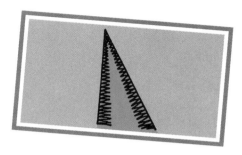

Re-position the fabric when you turn round to come back. The straight edge will stay on the outside of the shape.

Turning Curves

When working curves keep stopping with the needle on the outside of the curve in the fabric, lift the foot, shift fabric slightly, lower foot and continue. This may need to be done every few stitches if it is a really small curve. The stitches overlap on the inner edge of the curve leaving no gaps.

Points

Put the needle position to the right and narrow the zig-zag as you approach the point starting where the wider zig-zag would have overlapped. Leave a very small width at the point.

Hand Sewn Method

This is worked in a frame (see page 47). Prepare the fabrics and frame up the background fabric in a ring or frame.

If required tack the seam allowance under on each motif before the piece is applied to the background. On curved sections cut slits or V-shaped notches almost to the stitching line before turning the seam allowance under.

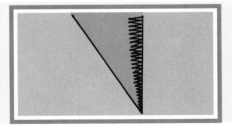

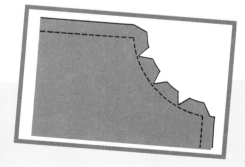

At the corners, snip straight across just

outside the seamline, turn under a tiny hem, then fold in the sides along the seamline and tack.

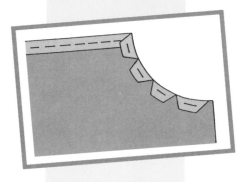

Pressing is optional - a pressed edge will look flat and sharp while an unpressed edge will look slightly raised.

Pin prepared motifs in position on the background fabric, matching the grain of the fabrics, using fine steel pins placed at right angles to the edges of the motifs. If the motif is large, tack it in place both horizontally and vertically, working from the centre.

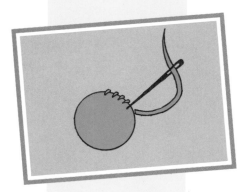

Using matching thread and a fine needle, stab stitch all round the edge as invisibly as possible. This edge can be embroidered over afterwards.

No-sew Method

Before the motifs are cut out, back the fabric to be applied with pieces of an adhesive nylon web following the manufacturer's instructions. Then mark and cut out the motif using methods already given or alternatively pencil round a reversed template of the motif on the paper backing. Cut along the pencilled line.

Peel off the backing paper. Position the motif on the prepared background material and iron in place following the manufacturer's instructions.

Pattern and Designs

Baby's Alphabet Quilt

Size

Finished measurement: 85 x 119 cm [35 x 49 ins]

Each square measures: 20 x 20 cm [8 x 8 ins] with 1.5 cm [$1/2$ inch] seam allowances.

Materials

60 cm [$5/8$ yard] 120 cm [48 ins] wide plain fabric.

60 cm [$5/8$ yard] 120 cm [48 ins] wide green floral fabric.

20 cm [$1/4$ yard] 120 cm [48 ins] wide blue gingham fabric.

20 cm [$1/4$ yard] 120 cm [48 ins] wide yellow striped fabric.

20 cm [$1/4$ yard] 120 cm [48 ins] wide light floral fabric.

130 cm [$13/8$ yards] 120 cm [48 ins] wide Backing fabric.

130 cm [$13/8$ yards] 120 cm [48 ins] wide polyester wadding, 2 cm [$3/4$ inch] thick.

Polyester sewing thread.

Templates

On the following pages 14 to 34 we have supplied all the letters of the alphabet, plus all the numerals. These are printed on a grid, of which each square represents 1 cm. To enlarge the letters or numbers to the correct size, draw on a piece of thick paper or thin card a grid with 1 cm squares, then transfer the design square by square, from one grid to another.

Once you have all the letters or numbers you require at the correct size cut the templates out so that they are ready to use.

Note: No allowances have been made for turnings on the letters supplied. If you require turnings remember to add them on when cutting the fabric.

Preparation

Cut 10 squares of plain fabric

9 squares of green floral fabric

6 squares of yellow striped fabric

6 squares of light floral fabric

4 squares of blue gingham fabric

From the plain fabric cut the letters B, E, G, H, J, K, L, M, N, O, P, Q, S, T, V and Y.

From the green floral fabric cut the letters A, C, D, F, I, R, U, W, X and Z.

Cut a piece of fabric 88 x 122 cm [36 x 50 ins] for the backing.

Also cut the polyester wadding to this size.

To make

Lay the squares out as shown above and place letters on the relevant squares. Pin, tack and then appliqué the letters on to the squares.

Once the letters are appliquéd to the squares, the squares must be joined. Taking care to ensure all the letters are the correct way up when the squares are joined, with right sides together join the side edges of each row of five squares. Press the seams open. Then with right sides together join the rows of squares together. Trim the seam allowances on intersecting corners (see page 42) to reduce bulk.

Tack the wadding to the wrong side of the joined squares.

With right sides together pin, then tack the joined squares to the backing fabric. Stitch around all four sides of the fabric leaving an opening along the bottom edge to turn the quilt through. Trim the corners.

Turn the quilt right side out through the unstitched edge at the bottom. Close the opening by slip-stitching.

From the appliquéd side of the quilt, stitch in the seam groove along the lines which form the edges of the squares. Stitch by machine, or by hand with a small running stitch, to make the squares stand out.

Design Variations

Harmony Class gives you all the information you need to make a quilt or playmat. Your finished quilt is likely to be unique even if it is made to the same pattern as given here because the fabrics you use will be different. The choice of fabrics is not the only way to create your own design. You may decide to change the shape or size. Rather than 5 rows of 7 squares you might have 6 rows of 6. Once

you have decided on the finished size you can choose what to appliqué on to the squares, whether it is letters, numbers or a combination of both.

The finished appearance of your quilt will largely depend on your choice of fabrics. You may decide to buy fabrics especially for the project or use up oddments.

There are two ways you can go about planning your design. The first is on paper with the shape of your quilt drawn on it and using coloured pencils similar to the fabrics you intend to use (see page 36 for a few suggested patterns). Alternatively you can start with a collection of fabrics cut into 20 x 20 cm [8 x 8 ins] squares. Arrange them on the floor or a table until you find a pleasing pattern then decide whether your fabrics would look more attractive with plain or patterned letters and in which position they would look best.

You may want to decorate the letters you have chosen like the C on page 17. We have given a few suggestions but they could also be embellished with embroidery.

On the following pages with all the letters and numbers, we have given you a selection of suggestions for quilts you could make but ultimately **the choice is yours!**

Designs

You may wish to use your own design, an illustration from a book, a postcard or a photograph as a motif. This might have to be scaled to the size you require.

Enlarging and Reducing Designs

Trace off the original design and enclose it in a square or rectangle as desired.

To Enlarge a Design

Place the original tracing on the bottom left hand corner of a sheet of paper, large enough for the final design. Starting at bottom left draw the exact diagonal line of the original and extend it across large piece of paper. Mark the required finished width along the bottom, and draw a vertical line from there up to the diagonal to give the height. From this point draw a line parallel to the base line. This gives both measurements of the required frame in exact proportion to the original. Make a grid as given below.

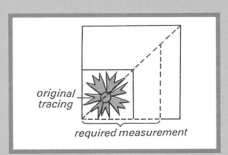

To Reduce a Design

Place required paper on original tracing and draw a diagonal across them both. Proceed as given for enlarging a design, but working on the reduction.

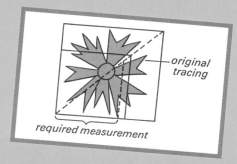

Divide both the tracing and the paper into an equal number of divisions. This can be done by folding and refolding the paper and then ruling along the lines. Number the squares of both grids starting from one corner. Transfer the design square by square from one grid to the other. The more detailed the design, the more squares there should be.

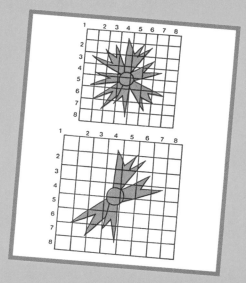

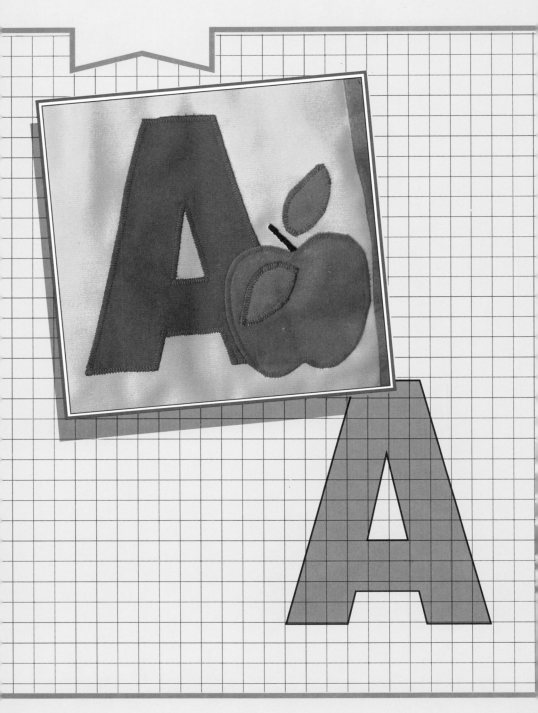

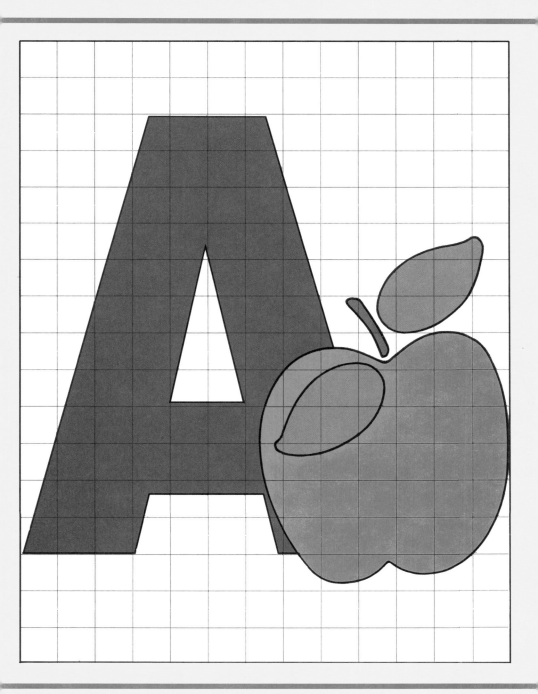

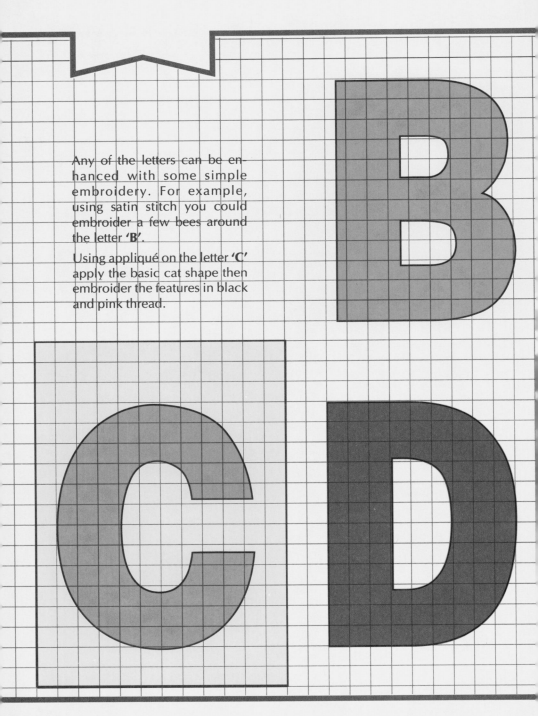

Any of the letters can be enhanced with some simple embroidery. For example, using satin stitch you could embroider a few bees around the letter **'B'**.

Using appliqué on the letter **'C'** apply the basic cat shape then embroider the features in black and pink thread.

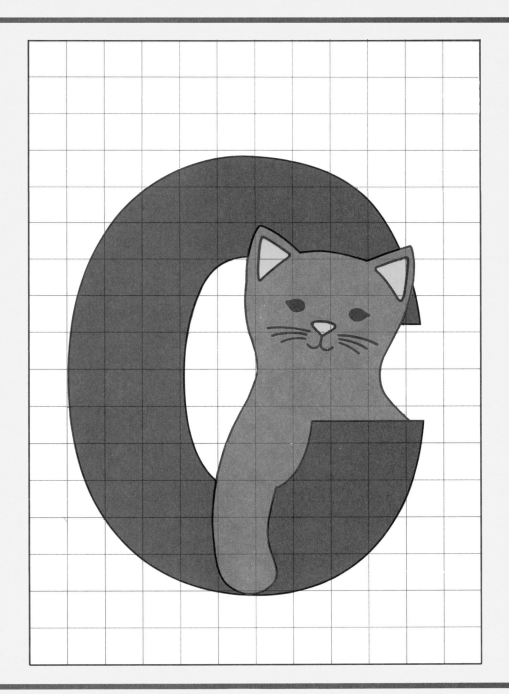

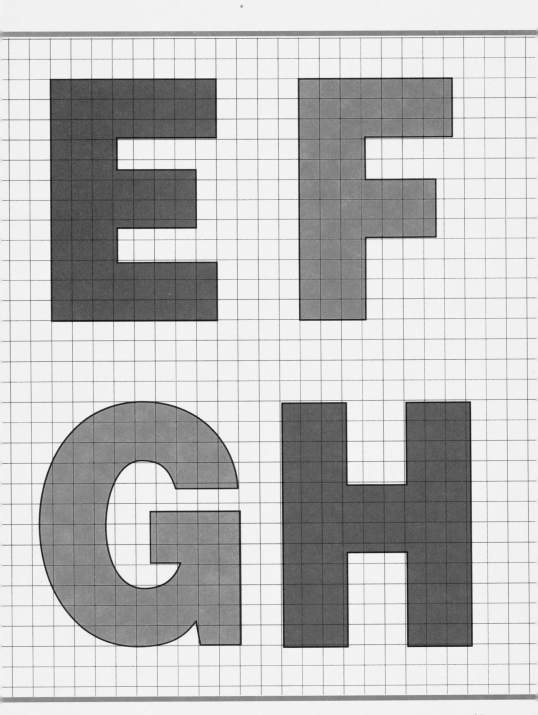

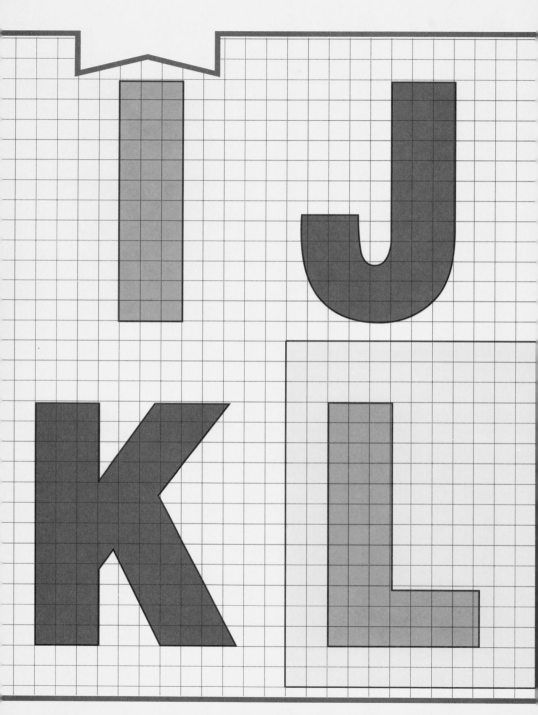

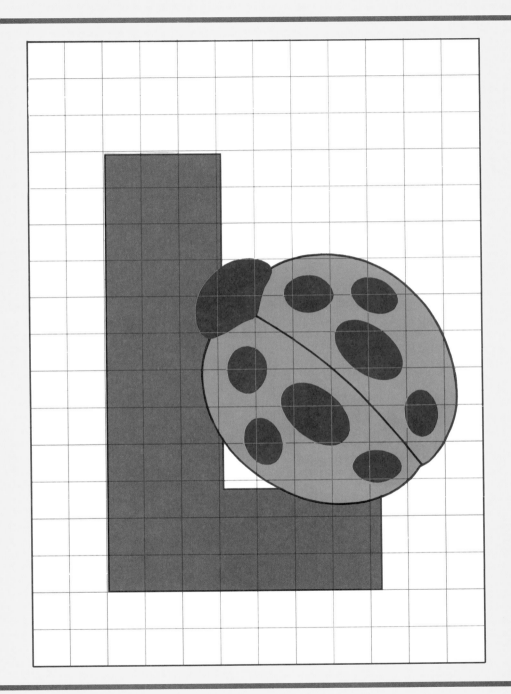

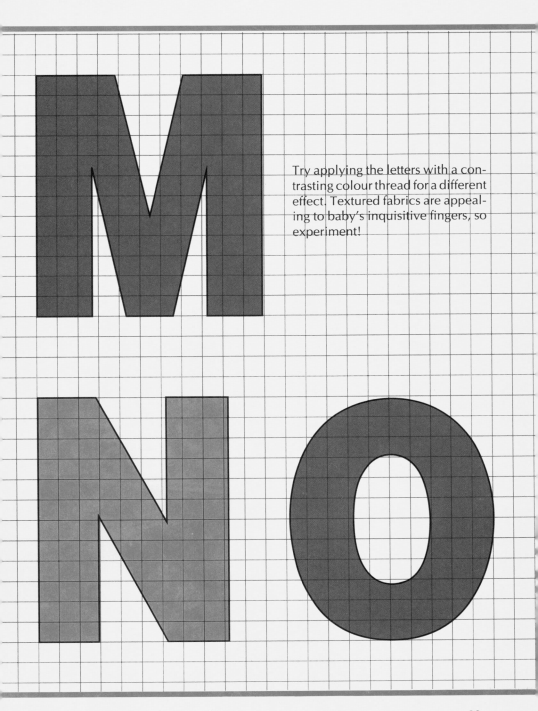

Try applying the letters with a contrasting colour thread for a different effect. Textured fabrics are appealing to baby's inquisitive fingers, so experiment!

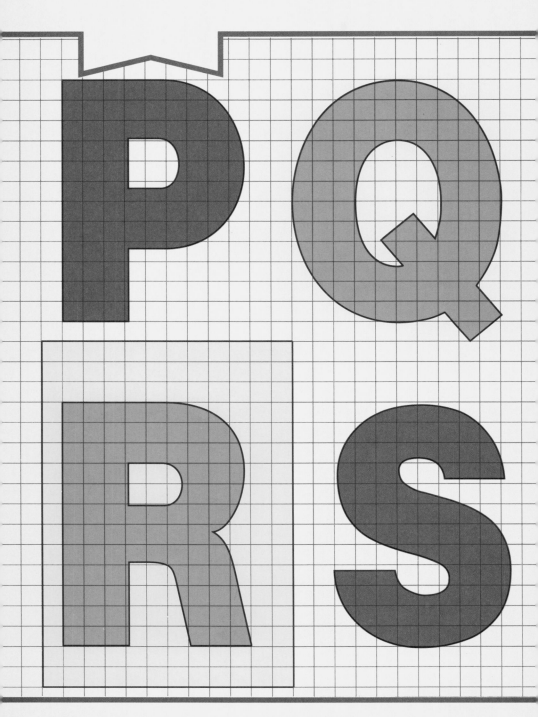

Children's books are an ideal source of inspiration for different Motifs that can be applied to particular letters.

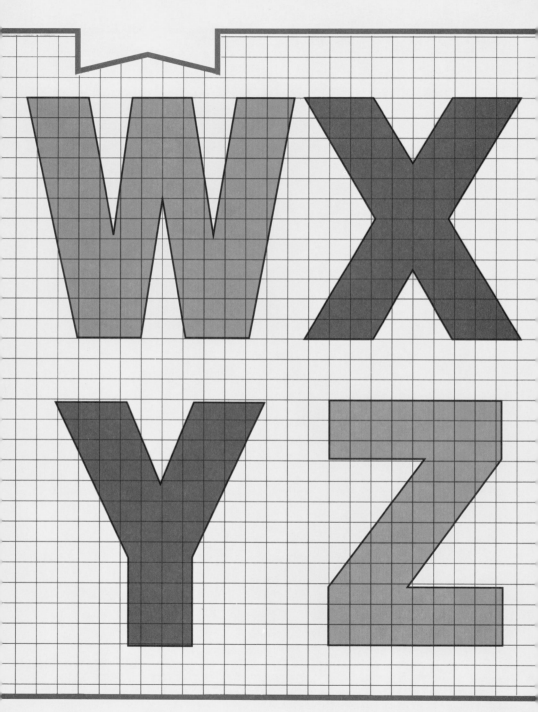

29

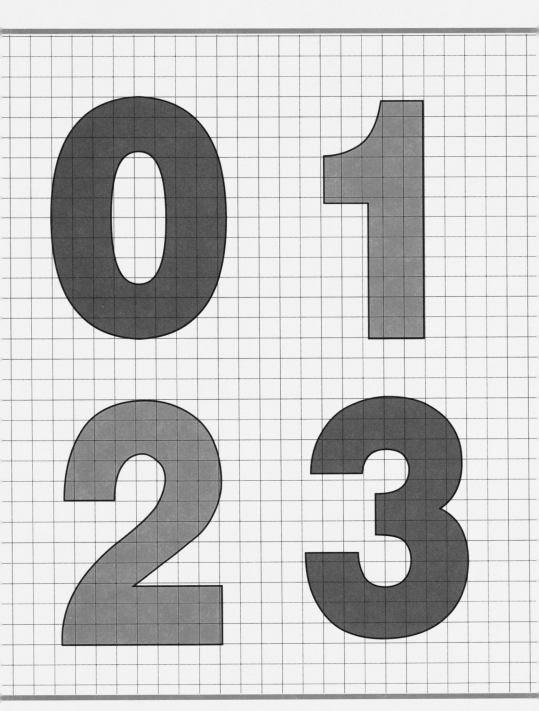

31

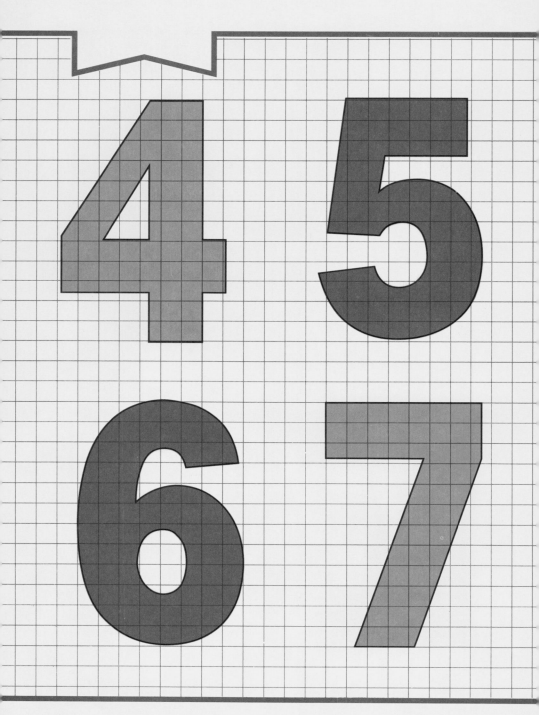

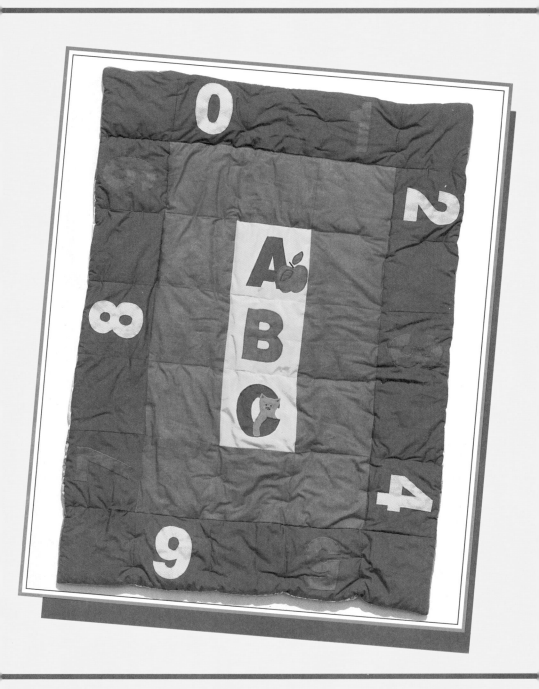

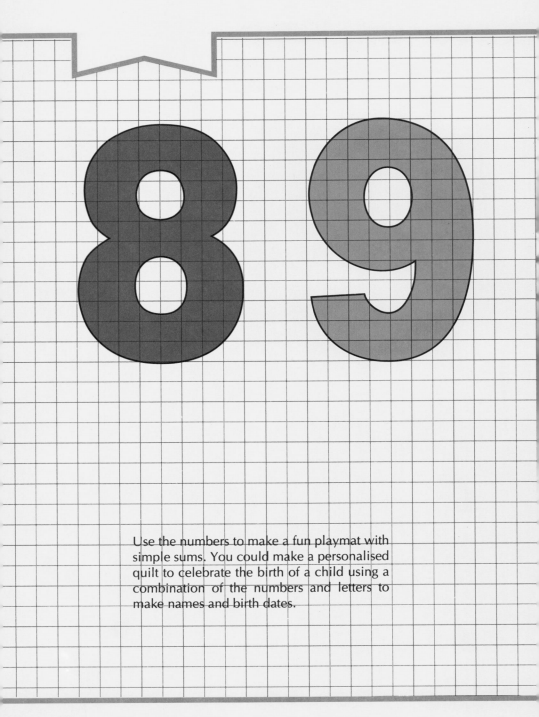

Use the numbers to make a fun playmat with simple sums. You could make a personalised quilt to celebrate the birth of a child using a combination of the numbers and letters to make names and birth dates.

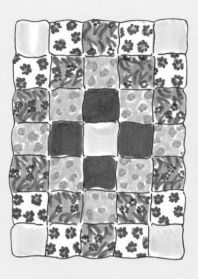

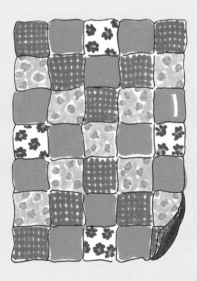

Here we show some ideas for colour arrangement - but your choice will depend on the fabrics you have available.

Sewing Know How

In the following pages we give information, instructions and diagrams for some basic sewing and embroidery techniques.

Equipment

Fabrics

As a general rule, natural fabrics such as cotton, linen and silk are the most suitable for appliqué and embroidery, although a small proportion of man-made fibre will make the fabrics easier to care for.

Threads

The type of thread you should use will depend on the fabric (it is better to use a cotton thread on a natural fabric) and the stitching requirements. Unless a contrasting thread is to be a feature, the thread you choose should be the same colour or a shade darker than your fabric. If you are using a plaid, print or tweed match the thread to the dominant colour in the fabric.

Tools

The basic tools of the trade will help to make your sewing as fast, easy and enjoyable as possible. Ideally you will need a selection of needles, pins, pin cushion, a thimble and several pairs of scissors. A small sharp pointed pair for snipping threads, a long-bladed pair for cutting out and an old pair for cutting card and paper.

Also useful are dressmakers pencils. These chalk-like crayons can be used to mark the fabric, the brush on the end is for removing the marks after use. It is, however, advisable to make marks on the wrong side of the fabric where possible.

Sewing Machines

A sewing machine is useful although not essential. Good quality stitching is dependent on having the correct tension, pressure, needle size and stitch length. Many machines now have a universal setting which is correct for most sewing jobs. But you may need to adjust it for some fabrics or sewing tasks. To ensure the best results always test stitch on off-cuts of the fabric you are using for your garment.

Thread Tension

When the tension is correctly set, the stitches should be perfectly balanced, the two threads interlocking in the centre of the fabric so that the stitches look the same on both sides of the fabric.

To test for balanced tension, thread the machine with different colour threads in the needle and the bobbin.

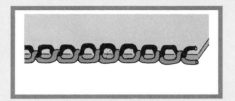

Take a scrap of fabric and fold it along the bias. Stitch a line about 1.5 cm [¹/₂ inch] in from the fold then pull the fabric until the thread breaks.

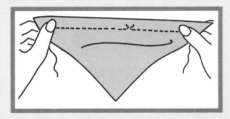

If both the bobbin and the needle thread break then the tension is correct.

If only the bobbin thread breaks that means that the bobbin tension is tighter than the needle tension.

To remedy, tighten the needle tension to match that of the bobbin.

If only the needle thread breaks, that means that the needle tension is tighter than the bobbin tension.

To remedy, loosen the needle tension to match that of the bobbin.

Stitch Length

The stitch length is easily changed on every machine. It is advisable to ex-periment for the most suitable stitch size on a scrap of fabric before sewing your project.

The weight of the fabric is important in determining the stitch length to be used. Generally the lighter the fabric the shorter the stitch length and the heavier the fabric the longer the stitch length. If the fabric has texture further adjustments may be required.

Guiding the Fabric

Use both hands to gently guide the fabric through the machine as you stitch. Do not push or pull the fabric. At the same time keep your eye on the cut edge of the fabric, rather than on the needle. This helps you to keep the stitching straight.

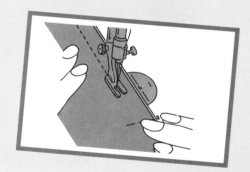

Accuracy

The easiest way to maintain accurate stitching is to align the right edge of the fabric with a guide line. You can use one of the lines etched in the plate on your machine or make your own mark with a piece of tape stuck on the plate at a measured distance from the needle hole. The edge of the foot is useful as a guide for stitching very close to an edge.

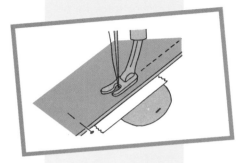

bites of fabric right at the seamline. The heads should be to the right of the presser foot so that they can be efficiently removed as you stitch.

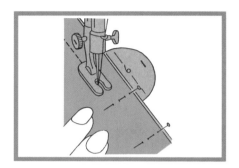

Securing the Stitching

To prevent the stitching from coming undone at the beginning and end of the seam, either back-stitch at both ends or tie the threads ends together.

Sewing Techniques

These are the basic methods of work required to complete a project.

Pinning and Tacking/Basting

There are several ways of holding the fabric layers in place prior to stitching and each depends upon the type of fabric or seam.

Pinning

This is the quickest and easiest method and fine for most seams.

Place pins at right angles to the seam-line, 2.5 to 7.5 cm [1 to 3 ins] apart. Insert the pins so that you take small

Machine Tacking/Basting

This is most often used to sew a fabrics together temporarily.

1 Pin the fabric in place.

2 Loosen the needle thread tension, adjust the stitch setting to the longest length, and stitch. Do not bother to secure the stitching at the ends of the seams.

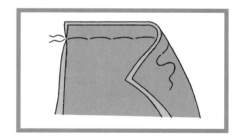

To remove the tacking easily, clip the needle thread every 2.5 cm [1 inch] or so, then pull out the bobbin thread.

Hand Tacking/Basting

Hand tacking is a secure method of holding fabric layers temporarily in place. It is frequently used in detail areas where pinning would not be accurate or secure enough and machine tacking would be difficult to do.

For the firmest holding power weave the needle in and out of the fabric so that the stitches and the spaces between them are all the same size - approximately 5mm [^{1}/$_4$ inch] long.

For areas that do not need to be so secure, make the stitches 5mm [^{1}/$_4$ inch] long and the spaces between 1.5 cm [^{1}/$_2$ inch] long.

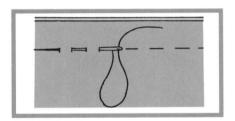

Plain Seams

With right sides together, stitch along the seamline, which is usually 1.5 cm [^{1}/$_2$ inch] from the cut edge. Press the seam allowances open.

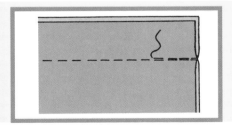

Corners

To strengthen seams at corners, shorten the stitch length for about 2.5 cm [1 inch] on either side of the corner. This reinforcement stitching helps to prevent the corner from fraying after it is trimmed and turned right side out.

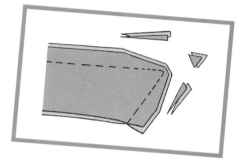

For sharp outward corners take one or two diagonal stitches across the point, instead of stitching right up to it. Trim across the point first then trim diagonally on either side.

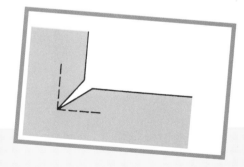

For inward corners reinforce with small stitches and clip to the stitching line.

Trimming and Clipping

It is vitally important to trim and/or clip certain seam turnings to give flatter edges, crisper corners, and smoother curves and seams. Also to eliminate excess fabric at the seam allowances of corners and points.

Intersecting Seams

When one seam or dart will be crossed by another, diagonally trim the ends of the first seam allowance or dart to reduce the bulk.

On outward, or convex curves, cut wedge-shaped notches from the seam allowance to eliminate excess fullness.

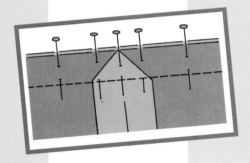

Pressing

To achieve the best results **press as you go**. Do not cross two seams without having first pressed the original seam open. Ideally your ironing board should be set up close to your sewing machine. Organise your sewing so that you work on several sections at one time, and then press everything that needs it at the same time.

On inward, or concave curves, make little clips or snips in the seam allowance just to, but not through, the stitching.

Always test the pressing method on a scrap of fabric before pressing the actual garment. Make sure the fabric is straight and as smooth as possible before starting. Remove pins before pressing, they could leave impressions on the fabric or damage the iron. Tacking/basting stitches can also leave impressions and so they should also be removed before pressing.

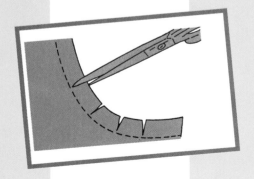

As a rule it is best to use light pressure, without resting the full weight of the iron on the fabric. Do **not** over press, you may damage the fabric and cause it to shine.

Top-stitching

This is an extra row of stitching on the outside of the garment along or near a finished edge. Although top-stitching is usually added as decoration, it can also be functional. For example, it can be used to attach a patch pocket or to help keep seam allowances flat on hard-to-press fabrics.

Use a matching or contrasting thread as desired. A thicker buttonhole thread could be used. Test the stitch on the same number of layers of fabric, with a slightly longer stitch.

To make each stitch more pronounced, slightly loosen the needle thread tension. It may also be necessary to adjust the presser foot pressure to accommodate the extra bulk.

Stitching in the Seam Groove

This technique is a quick way to hold layers of fabric in place at the seams.

Make sure the seam allowances have been pressed open. On the outside stitch in the groove formed by the seam, trying not to catch the fabric surface. Be sure to catch all the underneath layers in their correct position in your stitching.

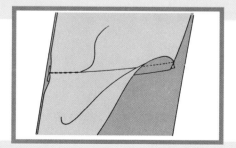

Hand Stitches

Backstitch

This stitch is used to secure beginnings and ends of hand sewn seams, as well as for repairing seams. There are many variations, but all are worked by inserting the needle into the fabric behind the thread.

1 With right sides of the fabric together fasten the thread on the underside of the fabric and bring the needle up through all the layers.

2 Insert the needle back down through the fabric, 2mm [1/8 inch] behind the point where it first emerged.

3 Bring the needle up again 2mm [1/8 inch] ahead of the first stitch. Continue along the length of the seam.

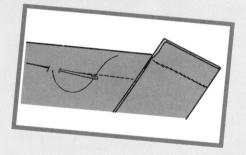

Running Stitch

This is used for gathering, tucking, mending and for seams that are not under strain.

Weave the needle in and out of the fabric several times before pulling the needle through the fabric. The stitches

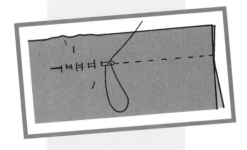

and spaces should be the same length, about 2 to 3mm [1/8 inch] in length for seams and twice as long for gathering.

Slip-stitch

This is used for securing all turned under edges, because the stitches are invisible on both the inside and outside of the garment.

1 Fasten the thread to the folded edge of the fabric. Then working from right to left, pick up a single thread in the garment just below the folded edge.

2 Insert the needle into the fold directly above the first stitch and bring it out 5mm [1/4 inch] away.

3 Pick up another thread in the garment directly below the point where the needle emerged and continue alternating between garment and fold.

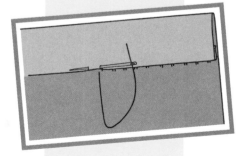

Embroidery Stitches

The addition of embroidery stitches to a garment can be a very effective form of surface decoration. It is especially popular on children's clothes, but can also give an individual finish to many other types of garment.

The use of a frame (see page 47) makes working embroidery stitches easier.

Blanket Stitch

This stitch can be worked over an edge as a method of finishing a raw edge. When used as a decorative stitch mark two parallel lines. Working from left to right, bring the needle out on the lower line, insert the needle on the top line, a little to the right. Bring it out on the lower line directly below, keeping the thread under the point of the needle pull the needle through.

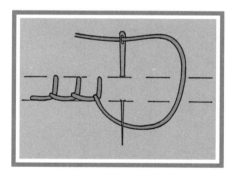

Chain Stitch

Bring the needle to the right side and working from right to left, looping the thread insert the needle where the thread emerges and bring it out a short distance away, keeping the working thread under the point of the needle.

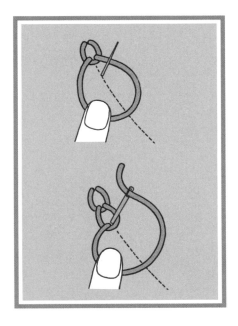

Cross Stitch

Bring the needle out at A, insert it at B, then out at C, and into D, repeat as required. To work the other diagonal bring the needle out at E, insert it at B and so on.

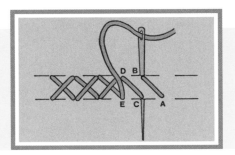

Detached Chain Stitch.

A single chain stitch is made and is secured by taking the thread over the loop and through the fabric.

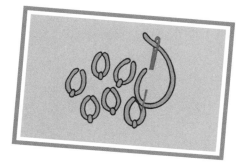

Feather Stitch

Bring the needle to the right side of the fabric and to the right of the marked line. Holding the thread, take a small diagonal stitch above the thread on the left of the line, repeat on the opposite side of the line. Continue, working on alternate sides of the line.

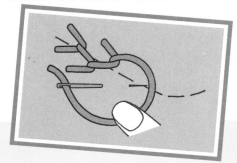

French Knot

Bring the needle to the right side, holding the thread down with the left hand, wrap the yarn around the needle twice, take the needle to the wrong side close to where it emerged and pull the thread through leaving a small knot.

the left (C), insert the needle at D and make a small stitch to the left (E).

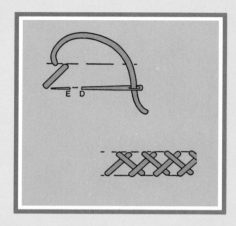

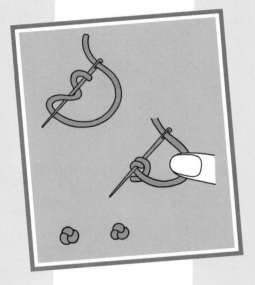

Lazy Daisy Stitch

The stitches are formed in the same way as chain stitch, but working from the centre and fastening each loop with a small stitch.

Herringbone Stitch

Working from left to right, bring the needle to the right side at A, insert the needle at B and make a small stitch to

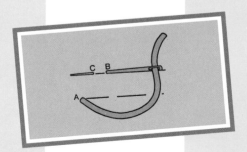

Satin Stitch

Work parallel straight stitches close together over the shape. A raised effect can be achieved by first working running stitches over the area.

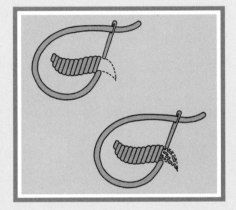

Stem Stitch

Working from left to right along the design line, bring the needle to the right side of the line, take a small stitch and return the needle to the left of the previous stitch.

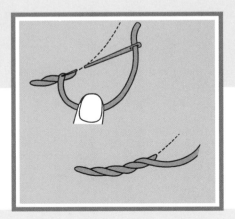

Frames

The Ring Frame is used for working small areas by hand and when doing free machine embroidery. It can be wood or metal and consists of two rings which fit together.

The inner ring should be covered with a crossway binding to prevent the embroidery slipping. The outer ring has a break in it and is held by a bolt and a tensioning screw. The fabric is laid over the inner ring and the outer ring is pressed over this, gripping the fabric between the two. The fabric is gently pulled taut and the tension screw is tightened to hold it in place.

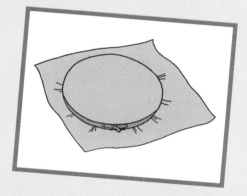

For hand embroidery the ring frame is used with the stretched fabric surface uppermost but it can, in fact, be used either way up. The right side of the fabric can be laid over or under the inner ring. Ring frames are always used 'upside down' on the sewing machine so that the fabric lies flat on the working surface.

Top of the Class

Hints and tips to help and improve your sewing.

To stitch perfect corners it helps to mark with chalk where the two seamlines intersect. Then stitch to this point and with the needle still in the fabric, raise the presser foot, pivot the fabric to the correct position to finish the seam, lower the presser foot and continue stitching.

To help prevent the motif fabric fraying whilst being handled, use a lightweight fusible interfacing on the wrong side, following the manufacturer's instructions.

It is important on any project to take care at every stage. To get the best results pin, tack, stitch and then press.

Once you have made one grid to the correct size either photocopy it the number of times you need it, or for each motif lay a piece of tracing or greaseproof paper over the grid and transfer the design on to this.

Added interest can be given to projects by cutting stripes and plaids on the bias.

If the stitching line or seam line will be intersected by another line of stitching don't secure the ends. The second row of stitching will secure the first row.

Try using textured fabrics to appliqué on to a baby's playmat, they create extra interest for inquisitive fingers.